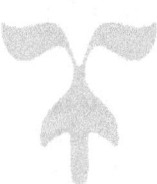

The Evolutionary Logic
Of
Liberation Psychotherapy

* * * * *

Human Nature
In the
Twenty-First Century

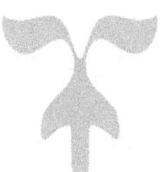

ISBN-13:
9781535544030
ISBN-10:
1535544031

DEDICATION:

To the curious, creative,
growing individuals
who keep contributing to
make this world
a better place,
&
In Loving Memory
of
David Swetman
and
Royann & Stan Cross
who used presuppositions
with love.

Table of Contents
(Pg. 4)

THE

EVOLUTIONARY

LOGIC

Of

LIBERATION

PSYCHOTHERAPY

* * * * * *

*Human Nature
In the
Twenty-First Century*

INTRODUCTION

I begin with definitions because of my firm belief that specificity leads to both clarity of understanding as well as providing the beginning of problem resolution. The following definitions will offer a more exact path to my entire thesis as is mirrored in the title of this monograph.

As for evolution, we know that life began around 3.8 billion years ago and has gradually changed over time to account for the billions of life forms on this planet. Our Homo-sapiens species came forth around 200,000 years ago and contains psychological remnants from previous lower animal species. Therefore, one of my first tasks is to discern ancient tendencies within each of us - said tendencies which affect both our thinking and behavior.

To explain "Logic" in the title, I provide a syllogism:
Evolved animals of all types have hard-wired instincts.
Homo sapiens are an evolved animal species.
Therefore, humans have instincts as part of their nature.

I will leave the greater definition of the word 'Liberation' to Chapter Seven, but, for now, recognition of evolutionary remnants does not mean being controlled by them. Rather, the accretion of new brain functions gained over hundreds of thousands of years happen to be available to our species. These new frontal lobe accretions mean that we have the power of decision. The trick is to decide out of the best available knowledge and not being guided by an old automatic instinct.

'Psychotherapy', in its Greek origins, meant the healing (therapy) of the soul (Psyche). The Soul, in this monograph, has no metaphysical connotation. Rather, I point to three soulful meanings:

1)   Soul is based on the human potential which grows from a peaceful and happy attachment to a healthy mother by a newborn. (*The qualification is that there were no genetic, addictive, or nurturing failures while the child was in the womb*). The healthy infant, warmly bonded to a mother, quite naturally exhibits six emotions: **sad** when food or nurture is missing, **anger** when treatment does not return the child to peace, **scare** of abandonment when the mother or a protective

known figure is missing - especially around seven to eight months, **happy** when all needs are met, leg-kicking *excitement* when favorite and familiar people, colors, and sounds are experienced, and *tender* in loving, giving and receiving moments. Each of these six emotions is primary to Liberation Psychotherapy. We see them as prime motivators in human psychology, though it must be said upfront, that frequently these six emotions are lost and damaged by childhood conditions.

2)   The second aspect of Soul revolves around five values – usually only spoken of in philosophical treatises. And yet, a baby can discern and appreciate colorful baubles indicative of Beauty, has a sense of authenticity or Truth, knows when there is unfair conditions or Justice denied (at its most basic level), both gives and receives kindness or Goodness, and is aware of Love which embraces the whole. Thus, Soul at both its beginning infantile expressions and later mature adult characteristics embraces Beauty, Truth, Justice, Goodness, and Love.

3)   The third expression of Soul must hearken back to the Greeks who consistently valued Reason. As we travel along understanding

instincts in this Monograph, it is vital to underscore – at the very beginning – that major decisions in life *must* come from employing our highest brain/mind functions. Otherwise, we could be battered around by aggressive or sexual instincts and lose our souls in the process.

All three of these major areas of Soul play significant roles in Liberation Psychotherapy. Furthermore, the three are the primary manifestations of the post-therapeutic adult.

Two Dominant Approaches to Soul-healing

Throughout recorded history in all societies of the world, two systems of healing have prevailed. The first can be encapsulated under the large rubric of Religion. Someone experiencing mental confusion approaches a priest (of whatever kind) and is instructed in a given faith. A believer is provided with a community, rituals, proverbs, secret writings, a discernment between sacred and profane, and instruction in morality. The premise is that the new believer, having accepted the prescribed religious path, will gain peace of soul and no longer be subject to the mental turmoil of the unbelievers. Here, I add a footnote: Humans do search for meaning and the acceptance of an ideology and community does provide a measure of succor.

The second system offering major help concerns itself with physical solutions. Historically speaking, human societies ever have the range of professionals ranging from witch doctors to brain surgeons. As culture and time passed, the treatments became far more sophisticated. Since the late Nineteenth Century, the psychiatric community has availed itself of the Diagnostic and Statistical Manual of Mental Disorders.

Both of the above systems begin with a father or mother figure that dispenses counsel, prescribes rituals, and – in most recent times – makes available legitimate drugs. Personally speaking, I do not quarrel with either system in terms of given situations. Religion around the world acknowledges the Golden Rule where we humans are to treat other humans the way we would prefer being treated. There are multiple examples of good proverbs, community gatherings, and comforting treatises which must be respected. By the same token, drugs are necessary for some conditions (schizophrenia) and provide instant help for other situations. Therefore, my tendency is to analyze what is best for what condition and go from there.

Most of all, I rather despise fundamentalism of any type. Fundamentalism has the smug premise that their way is the only right way.

I have called attention to the above two systems in order to show the difference of approach characteristic of Liberation Psychotherapy. We do not accept the role of counseling father or mother, nor do we have rapid prescriptions. In fact, Lib Psych is not prescriptive with instantaneous help. Stance-wise, Liberation Psychotherapists accept a peer-to-peer style where two equal humans are working together to figure things out. We do not give advice or provide pharmaceuticals. Our system is dynamic in that it continually refers to the fluid six primary emotions naturally infused in the human mind and body. We know that instincts leave individual Homo-sapiens enormously varied, instinctually driven, and rationally creative so all interventions must deal with complexity. There are no easy solutions. Rather, each session is creative, and because of knowledge of internal emotional dynamics, quite exciting.

To stretch understanding of Liberation Psychotherapy a bit further than just animal instincts, I underscore that our operational premises are that we humans all have adaptations leftover from childhood situations, childlike reasoning, and childlike decisions. One understanding arising to the surface by recognizing the power of adaptations since birth is that all families and all individuals (including parents) are dysfunctional in some way or another. When people rely upon sheer reason to figure out human dysfunction, they run into stone walls of confusion. In Lib Psych, the attitude is this: *We are all in this together, and using the best thinking of both of us, we will figure out a path to a good, happy, and psychologically free life*

A Primary Illustration

Pictures are better than words. Readers need a visual illustration of how a person's identity and relationships are drastically affected by childhood thinking errors which continue in adult life. I will focus on my own family and my Mother's psychology because I was able to closely observe her for over sixty-five years. Dorothy Reinhardt Morris was both a tragedy and a victory – tragedy because so much of her life was a repeat of childhood and victory because, all in all, she was a good person. She died at age ninety-six in 2007. At her funeral the clergyman spoke of her "deep faith" (news to me!), service to the community (true enough), love of family (with certain qualifications), and her powerful personality. (You better believe it!) A granddaughter spoke of how "Granny" was approachable and fun, always had a full cookie jar, and taught her how to knit and crochet. A friend from the Rest Home said how "Dot" prepared secret care packages for fellow patients going through a crisis. A duet sang a hymn, the organ played softly, and the pastor ended with a prayer. All this was good, nurturing, and socially appropriate – a decent public way to say Goodbye to my Mom. But, **nothing** was said about what went on behind closed doors.

The truth is rather unpleasant. My Mother had a destructive Script which helped ruin her marriage, psychologically hurt two of my brothers, and left one son (me) puzzled by the multiplicity of personalities Dorothy Reinhardt Morris exhibited. It is true that she was generally happy about life, eager to do well in the community, and quite loving with members of the family. Then, BAM! Some switch occurred and she went into hateful mode. If she had appeared at the pastor's office for help, she would have been consoled and prayed over. If she had gone to a psychiatrist, she would have been tranquilized. As I, the middle observant child, witnessed her behavior, I was really puzzled.

A Lib Psych therapist would have inquired about Dorothy's childhood. She was born in May 1911 and her sister Mildred was born on 12/12/12. Those close births resulted in a horrible sibling rivalry which was shockingly exhibited over ninety years! The sisters went at each other with hateful words and destructive generalizations. If anyone interrupted their routine (which I termed The Dot and 'Mit' Show) they would change their voices, laugh, and declare us kids crazy for thinking they was any enmity "because we love each other." In one way, they did. Otherwise, we kids were scarred by their repetitive hatefulness.

Furthermore, the Dot and 'Mit' routine did not end with just each other. At times, each of them turned on the old bile to their children, grandchildren and even neighbors. Chief to be scorned were their husbands. My mother could spew forth hatred to my father in intimacy-destroying manners, which was extremely sad to me. I early realized both sisters had a favorite and a scorned person as roles in their Dot and 'Mit' Show. To further this analysis, both my mom and aunt would spring their Script when faced with a dyad – someone was bad and someone good.

If there had been honest appraisals at my Mother's funeral, there would be an array of generalizations:

The Chosen Child: "Mom was an intelligent and loving human."

The Un-chosen, unworthy child: "She was a nasty bitch who always picked on me."

The Rest Home Administrator: "Dorothy was not a taker; she was a contributor."

My father: "She was sometimes loving and sometimes mean."

My Aunt 'Mit': "Dot could never get over my being born."

A Doctor: "This patient was quite neurotic.

An honest Pastor: "I never knew when she would be praising or critical."

Me, her invisible middle son: "I loved my Mom even though I recognized her varying mental states."

I provide a Benediction to this sad case study.

The moving Finger writes; and having writ,
moves on:
Nor all thy Piety or Wit shall lure it back to
cancel half a line.
Nor all the tears wash out a word of it.
                                    Omar Khayyam

A System Explanation

To have a respectable scientific system, it is necessary to have fundamental *Basic Units* upon which to empirically build a given theory. Chemistry has the Table of Elements and physics has the Four Forces. The building blocks of Liberation Psychotherapy are the previously mentioned hard-wired emotional instincts of Sadness, Anger, Scare, Happiness, Excitement, and Tenderness. The acrostic is SASHET. No one can understand, nevertheless respect Liberation Psychotherapy without knowing those six emotions. Primary to understanding are the abilities to recognize, communicate, and express these six emotions. They underlie all therapeutic understandings and interjections by therapists.

Students of human history well know how major disruptions and individual dysfunctions are caused by a failure to understand evolutionary instincts in general and evolutionary emotional instincts in particular. In the above illustration, there was no knowledge whatsoever of the emotional scare trigger which put the Dot and 'Mit' Show on stage. Those who know Lib Psych would have inquired, "What was the little one year old girl scared about, and what decisions did she make"? Such questions would have short-circuited the Staged Act and could have led to meaningful resolution. Therefore, once again, I underscore how utterly non-negotiable it is to omit the basic SASHET units. Those six provide lights along the path and they give the promise of meaningful hope.

Darwin and Evolutionary Psychology

The logic of Liberation Psychotherapy is traceable to Charles Darwin's The Origin of the Species which was published in 1859. While I have struggled with applications of evolution for over a half century, it has only been recently that I studied texts of the burgeoning field of Evolutionary Psychology. EP was not an available discipline when I was in universities, but, since about 1985, it has filtered into more and more colleges as a respectable study. I have been intrigued at how EP emphasizes the continuance of instincts in the mind of man, the existence of modules which affect our thinking and behavior, and how one can only understand Human Nature by beginning with biology. While I applaud and agree with those three emphases, I differ in several regards. Evolutionary Psychologists stop their analyses when it comes to influences after birth. Dramatically, that is where Liberation Psychotherapy has its major emphases. Also, I use the word "modularity" a bit differently, though for human reality re. Brain expressions, the definitions rather match. Furthermore, I have seen little recognition on the part of Evolutionary Psychologists to emphasize the instincts of emotion – my prime concern in psychotherapy. I happen to believe strongly that the dynamic triggering the old remnant instincts in the human mind is one of the six primary emotions. I also honor the practice of using case studies of live humans in psychotherapy to be empirically valid *when viewed in-masse and not just a singular recording.* Evolutionary Psychologists give little validity to case studies.

Thus, among three books Darwin wrote specifically on evolution, (<u>Origin</u>, <u>Descent</u>, and <u>Expressions</u>), I found <u>The Expressions of Emotions in Men and Animals</u> to be my prime source. Three examples: The maternal instinct of mammals is fierce when protecting her offspring. In therapy, I learned that the maternal instinct unleashed when a baby was born could mean the mother switches her love energy from her husband to the vulnerable infant. This had the potential to cause sexual problems with the spouse. A second illustration is the aggression impulse remnant in human personality. If humans do not recognize this old reflexive module built on both scare and anger, massive problems can occur. The third example is our sexual urges we inherit from our animal forbears. All manner of harmful expressions can occur ranging from rape, to sexual obsessions, to wild "tough sex" where a person regresses totally to an animal past. In sum, knowing our repressed animal instincts, and taking charge of them in socially appropriate manners, grants new measures of mental freedom.

A Philosophical Maxim

Over the decades I have relied upon an old maxim: "Anything can be used for anything." The amazing creativity granted Homo sapiens, means we can learn from or twist any natural instinct. We will have Rationalizations with us always. I cite this old proverb in order to acknowledge, up front, that each biological instinct is capable of misuse, or capable in freeing our minds to create beauty, truth, justice, goodness, and love. It is up to us.

A monograph cannot contain all the complexities humans lead us into. I must hit the highpoints even as my mind flits to deeper illustrations of a given client who was an exception to the rule. It remains true, however, that no client escaped the reality of SASHET. Of course, that meant scraping off the rationalization 'dirt' as we went deeper and more closely to the instinctual core. I will include as many specifics as I can in a small writing. I ask for your indulgence when a perfectly legitimate question pops into your mind and I have not provided an adequate explanation.

I pause to thank my reader/editor/ friends who have graciously offered their comments along the way. I, of course, assume responsibility for all errors. The following have done their best with me: Gary Brunson, Jaime LaRue, Mary Kay Walsh, Mary Sullivan, Chris Channer, Jim

Garden, Bob Hill, and my inimitable partner, Dix
Gescheidle Morris.

*Dix prefers to be in the shadows in this writing. I
still have a conscience module which strikes later
when I imply that the Lib Psych system was
created by me, alone. Nothing could be further
from the truth. And, maybe once again, I need to
accept responsibility for any mistakes, because in
my mind and experience, Dix is darn near perfect.*

Chapter One

The Entrance to Understanding Human Nature: EMOTIONS

Missing from my reporting on my Mother's ugly display of sibling rivalry was my Father's involvement in the whole dysfunctional scheme. Without even knowing Freud's term - 'Transference', you would automatically glean that Mom's scorn of him happened to be a little girl furious at how her mother and father had switched large amounts of their tender love to her sister Mildred. Those dynamics are clear in my mind – painfully so. However, my Father was not an innocent victim in their frequent shouting matches. Ernest Stephen Morris displayed what Evolutionary Psychologists call "mating anxiety" and "mate retention" – both of which are ancient reflexes from our animal heritage. The idea is that a male animal fears that his mate will run off with another animal. Call it what you will, one or the other would initiate shouting matches which left me scared about their repetitious scene.

Only on one occasion did their verbiage reach the level of semi-violence. At a Sunday breakfast when I was five years old, my Father initiated their screaming fits. "Well, who are you going to meet in church today? Who is your boyfriend going to be?" Mom dropped her fork and said loudly "You are crazy!" He threw a piece of bacon in her face, and she responded by dashing her orange juice in his face. Both furiously stood up as if to exchange blows and my older brother, Johnny, ran out of the room and returned with a rifle he aimed at my Father. I was utterly terrified. Mom told Johnny to put down the gun (which he did) and nothing more was said. The rifle disappeared from our home and we never had another gun in the house. I remained terrified, said terror which led to my lifetime of figuring out human psychology.

The Hidden World of Emotions

I was thirty-five when I began to suspect that emotions provided the keys to human nature. Without reciting major learning stages, I will simply plunge in to major discoveries Dix and I made when we did psychotherapy together. Beginning in 1975 we were co-therapists for thirteen group therapy sessions per week. We figured out the SASHET scheme and pursued the troubles of clients by following emotional clues throughout their lost mental wanderings. Let me cite some of our findings.

a) We saw that anger was a natural evolution-granted legitimate emotion which needed to be authenticated by both sexes. Therefore, we allowed clients full reign in following how their bodies wanted to express the feeling.

b) We encouraged clients to allow their sadness to come forth in crying, sobs, and even snotty nose running – we made it clear that authentic expression was perfectly all right with us.

c) We saw how scare combines choked breathing while making negative future visualizations. We taught people how to shake that emotion out of their bodies, breathe fully, and stay in the here-and-now.

d) Dix and I also learned how tenderness was blocked because clients reasoned, "If someone knows how I tenderly love them, they may abandon me and I would be devastated."

Our group therapy sessions were fantastically alive. Dix and I were seeing three major matters that I underscore for readers: 1) Releasing old traumatic wounds by making full sound, full bodily movement, and full breathing was introducing new freedom in the lives of clients. 2) By installing the six emotions in their relationships with their spouse and children, positive growth occurred.   3) Clients felt more together and more harmoniously peaceful when they had awareness of SASHET as they moved along with their lives.

Emotional Exercise

Clients were making emotional progress, but – at one point – I realized that they were not catching the SASHET emotions as they appeared in their bodies as quickly as I thought was good for them. So, to cement the six emotions into their minds by being aware of muscles involved, I introduced a new procedure at our group therapy sessions: "Everyone stand up. I will demonstrate where one of the emotions is felt in the body, and then I want you to copy me." (It was like an exercise class!) I would go through each of the 6 emotions, making sound, breathing into the emotion, and making appropriate gestures so everyone would get the idea. They followed and, as a result, greater progress in therapy was forthcoming.

Sadness occurs when someone experiences a loss (such as death) or is missing something (homesickness). It can be seen in a downcast head, stooped shoulders, and dismay in the eyes with orbicular muscles drawn in, lower lip exaggerated, and the voice rather forlorn. The therapist notes the sad signs and says softly…"Tell me about your loss or what you are missing."

Anger is revealed in glaring threatening eyes, clinched fists, hardened muscles, and the readiness to strike as if on the attack. The therapist says: "Tell me about how you or someone you care about has been threatened or discounted."

Scare is exhibited in tighter breathing, darting eyes, possible trembling as if to run, and a rather shaky voice. The person is ready to fight or flee.

Panic occurs when the brain has insufficient oxygen. The therapist says, "Share with me your fantasies about the future, as you note how your breathing has tightened."

Happiness appears in the lightness of one's musculature, the readiness to smile, a sense of peace and joy with a willingness to skip uncontrollably, open trusting appearance of one's face, and a sense of hopefulness. The therapist smiles and says "Tell me about your joy."

Excitement is shown in thrilling anticipation as the body wants to move more quickly, the voice make exulting sounds, the gestures become more exaggerated, and the person looks eagerly towards the future. The therapist says "Tell me about your anticipations."

Tenderness has the body go softer along with the voice, a sense of hugging and being close, and a reaching out as if to kiss. As said earlier, adults fear this emotion because of vulnerability which might lead to abandonment. The therapist encourages this emotion by making caring comments and speaking softly.

Deep Rapport

In the great main, emotions are not on the surface due both to childhood repressions and ordinary society being a bit cautious about 'emotional displays.' This means therapists must employ a bit of mind-reading, but not mystical mind-reading. Rather, therapists learn to identify with the client's body, breathe as the client breathes, set one's arms and legs in similar positions, and make very small gestures which mirror the client's movements. This process leads to exquisite rapport, which, in turn, leads therapists to know what a client is feeling in terms of the six emotions, before the client is aware of inner sensations.

The Function of Emotions

Our animal ancestors learned over long eons that survival meant encountering and solving daily problems involved the need for immediate solutions. Thus, the cattle prods of the SASHET emotions were installed in our viscera by the means of Natural Selection. A 'prod' of emotions led to adaptations in ways that guaranteed survival. Therefore, it is non-negotiable in terms of learning emotions. Vitality, and even life necessitated, for instance, seeing a poisonous snake meant a stab of scare followed by immediate safe movement away from the danger. Again, the six emotions evolved as signals alerting animals to an appropriate active response in a given situation. And, yes, this meant excitement in terms of sexuality and continuing one's species.

Inauthentic Human Emotional Adaptations

It would be ideal if a person's face automatically showed the inner emotions, but, alas, that seldom happens. (If the person was authentic about emotions, he/she would probably not have shown up for therapy!)

Therefore, we must consider four expressions which can lead therapy off on unproductive paths, but paths which prove quite productive once one understands. While one cannot verify these four in terms of our evolutionary animal past, the fact is that humans, using age-appropriate thinking, do in fact employ one of these.

Copied: Here a person mimics the body and emotions of another person. Ordinarily, this may be rather benign, but in some cases recognition of this faux expression is critical. For example, we saw several clients who had installed in their own bodies the displayed emotion of a parent. A boy, for instance, may copy his father's anger rages. A newborn girl may ingest her mother's post-partum depression and begin a lifelong drudging sadness. By knowing this category therapists can unlock some previously closed doors as a client is instructed how he/she is vicariously acting out a parent's problem. We found this knowledge to be quite helpful.

Manipulative: A child – when an adult, may continue a faux practice that worked with mom or dad and think their emotional expression is authentic when, in point of fact, it is not. Here the therapist must be a little careful because a person engaged in being The Happy Guy, or the Excited Princess (or whoever) may well defend the play as real. We found it helpful to say, "When you did this emotion with your mother or father, how did it work for you?" As the client learns that the display is inauthentic, therapists immediately say how the emotion was part real, but a child learned to exploit it. (Here again, the notion of "parts" or "modules" is quite important.)

Old / Repressed: This category is the largest of all because the truth is that everyone and every client frequently displays a traumatically stuck emotion *but has no awareness whatsoever that their expression is actually a demonstration of an old unresolved situation from childhood.* Thus, it becomes second nature for a therapist to inquire "How young do you feel when you experience that emotion?" Remarkably – and almost unbelievably – clients will immediately say a definite age. The therapist then follows a set of questions which I termed 'The Anatomy of a Trauma'. I will recite them in order:

1) The Original Situation: "Tell me what was going on back then from the standpoint of a scientific observer - as to: Place, Time, Circumstances, and Characters.

2) The Child's Perception. "What did the child see, hear, feel, and think?"

3) The Catastrophic Fantasy. "What terrible thing did the child imagine?"

4) The Child's Need or Want. What did the child need or want? "What want was buried?

5) The Blocked Emotional Expression. "What emotion was blocked?"

6) The Child's Mental Linkage. "What was going through the child's mind?"

7) The Fateful Decision. "What decision was locked in the child's thinking?"

8) The Body's Storage. "Where did you lock that situation in your musculature?

In the mid-1970's, I submitted 'The Anatomy of a Trauma' to a Psychological Journal. It was refused because an editor said Psychology was not Biology. I smile at that because the Anatomy of a Trauma has been used for decades in thousands of situations and has proven very effective – Biology or not!

Mechanisms of Defense

I add this section to our list of inauthentic emotional responses with the understanding that the defense procedure involves thinking and, interestingly enough, the refusal to feel authentically. These automatic old leftover procedures from childhood provide masks to actually feeling the **SASHET** emotions as they honestly emerge in a person's being. I list a few with the background of human development. Also, I emphasize again that a person is an assemblage of many mental parts and is not to be encapsulated in one expression, one diagnostic category, or one massive unthoughtful generalization.

Denial often begins with a birth trauma or a

mother's incapacity to provide sufficient caring nurture for a newborn. The infant responds by turning off his/her natural emotions because they only exacerbate the situation. Those with a six to eighteen month negative situation (my mother) **project** their negative emotions (sad, anger, scare,) on others. During the two year old phase, a child may major in **discounting** others thinking and being, as the little boy or girl thinks he/she is smarter than the parents. (This procedure of "Yes, but..." is one path to being a college professor.) Children three to six develop a **magical/fantasy** defense where authenticity of emotion is refused

'Mechanisms of Defense' is a very large subject and readers can look the options up online. Greatest among them is probably rationalization which, as we will learn in the chapter on consciousness, is the fallback position for people who handle their lives in a self-justifying manner. They live in the delusion that their thinking is reasonable and right, and others are at least a half bubble off from being level minded. I feel sad as I write this paragraph because rationalization destroys honest communication. However, rationalization is rampant in politics, religion, economics, and – in point of fact – the sine qua non of all ideologies. Far preferable for a vital life is to learn to recognize evolution's prompts within (i.e. SASHET), openly communicate those six emotions in a confessional manner, and express them as they are appropriate (and in private when you feel like screaming at the false communication in which society seems to dwell.)

Two Personal Stories

At age thirteen I went for help from my local pastor, Rev. J.G. Lott. With leaden feet, total breathless bodily dread, shaky tear-filled eyes and a fearful voice, I told him of my parents' verbal fights and asked if he would counsel them. His answer destroyed my hopes: "I don't get involved in family stuff. Get your father to come to church and believe in Christ. I am going fishing." And, with that said, he put on an old hat replete with fishing hooks, grabbed his fishing rod, and left the office. I sat there crushed. He was my only hope. I fell into despair.

But then I decided that, some day, I would figure things out. If I had approached our family doctor, Dr. R.F. Bonner, he would have suggested taking medicines to calm their nerves. Neither religion nor medicine would have made solid psychological interventions which would have calmed the rages of my original home.

For twelve years (1963-1975) I was a pastor in Chicago and environs. Though short on belief, parishioners accepted me because I was a good person to talk with. I listened, listened, listened. All the while the experiences of parishioners were sinking into my mind as I kept recognizing people had parts. The first neighborhood I served happened to be on the South Side of Chicago. In 1969, the first black family moved into the community, and, as a pastor, I visited Floyd who lived two doors down from the new black cop and his family.

Floyd knew my intention, and using churchly rhetoric said to me "Reverend, you don't have to worry about me. I know that in America people who work have a right to live wherever they want." He paused, and then Floyd said with a much harsher voice as he looked intently into my eyes, "But if that black bastard sets one foot on my lawn, I will cut his black ass in half with my 30-30! Do you understand me?!" Well, to confess, at that time I did not know modularity and quickly decided that Floyd was a hopeless racist.

As time went on, I learned people had multiple minds, and if I were to be effective as a therapist, I had best employ that information.

Chapter Two

Evolutionary Instincts

Definition: "Instinct or innate behavior is the inherent inclination of a living organism towards a particular complex behavior." *Wikipedia*

A lunch observation: "At the table behind me, I heard a four month old child give a sudden cry of alarm. The mother, sitting with a friend, said, "That's a wet diaper cry." She immediately changed the diaper, and the child went back to a peaceful and curious state. A lot of lessons were contained in those two acts of a baby's cry and a mother's response. In the following section you will be able to discern the innate actions.

A List of Instincts

In Darwin's Expression of Emotions in Men and Animals a list of several animal universals, which are independent of thinking and will power, are provided: blushing, yawning, perspiring, making sounds, weeping, frowning, sulking, shyness, sneering, tickling laughter, shrugging, surprise, disgust, the seeking of liquids and nurturing food, and, of course, sadness, anger, scare, happiness, excitement and tender love. For mammals there is the addition of suckling which infant animals of all types do without instruction. Each one of Darwin's list is untaught and appears rather automatically. With just these instincts in mind, all of us may be reminded of Walt Whitman's famous poetic phrase "I am large, I contain multitudes."

To Darwin's 1871 list we can add the following instincts:

The Life instinct to avoid death and stay alive
The acquisitive instinct
The maternal instinct to protect and serve infants
The building a nest instinct
The competitive instinct
The cooperative instinct
The empathy instinct based on mirror neurons
The instinct to fear strangers
The imitation instinct
The learning language instinct
The Tribal loyalty instinct
The Family loyalty instinct
The Innate curiosity to learn, instinct
The urge to play instinct
The territorial protection instinct
The creative instinct

The enjoyment of fantasy instinct
The instinctual fear of incest
The automatic fear of snakes and spiders
The sexuality instinct
The fear of abandonment instinct
The enjoyment of stories, instinct

All of the above and many still being recorded by Evolutionary Psychologists happen to be genetically wired innate responses of the lower animals and human animals. They are the product of eons of Natural Selection and they are imbedded in our viscera and brain/minds. If the goal is to understand Human Nature, every honest theorist must take the vast number of instincts into consideration because they are part and parcel of who we are. Any theory – religious, philosophical, sociological -biological, etc. – must include these instincts or it will fail from the very outset. In terms of medical diagnosis where a patient is placed in one mental disorder category, the reality is that old nineteenth century scheme must be updated. We can no longer think we understand human phenomena based on Reason alone.

Applications

Entire theories are built around one or more of the

instincts listed above. A dominant neo-liberal economic theory is built around competition, greed, and self-interest. A fundamentalist Christian sect may only note anger and aggression which are labeled as SIN. Humanistic theories about human nature may focus on empathy, compassion, and cooperation. Since anything can be used for anything, even SASHET can be seen as polarities where either excitement or scare is emphasized, happiness avoids the reality of sadness, and anger or tenderness comes to the fore as the only viable way to go.

The great number of instincts we inherited as the most astute conscious animal means that our mentality is divided with each of us having ambivalent tendencies pulling us in various directions. Liberation Psycho-therapy adds to the complexity by showing how SASHET can be misused by Copying, Manipulations, Regressive old states and even the Mechanisms of Defense. To be sure, all of this is difficult to balance, but in point of fact happens to be necessary if we want to deeply understand Human Nature in the 21st Century. Furthermore, mental health demands our knowing the truth. Looking back over the list of installed instincts in our makeup, none of us can voice an innocent "Moi?", to admitting we are evolved animals. We are. There is no question about it if we go by empirical evidence. So, yes we are sexual and aggressive creatures, both meek and courageous, both empathic and competitive, both acquisitive and greedy, and sharing, and on through the list. We contain multitudes. I must add that acknowledgement of truth always brings a measure of liberation to our souls.

A Recurrent Scare of Mine

Several parts of the above list do come to bear on my historical being, parts that I do not admire. At times in my journey I have been too aggressive, too taken by a territorial imperative, too expressive of anger-become-hate. While still a boy I would get into fist fights and break out into happy laughter as if my opponent and I had just fled propriety and were dealing with the real. When I played football as a teenager, I not only wanted to block and tackle properly, I wanted to hurt the other player – physically injure. I have had moments when giving a speech where I wanted to lambast sorry thinking, quaint harmful ideologies, and verbally annihilate some right wing nut. I experience this part of me as scary.

Do I have these evolutionary instincts under control? I'd say over 99.99 per cent because I am a cultured man, a person who champions Reason, and the fact is – I rather like people and like being liked. But, when I see Mitch McConnell on TV I have the urge to slap him. When Paul Ryan champions Reaganomics, I want to bear-hug him until he shouts "Uncle!" When I see white-shirted self-righteous Mormon missionaries, part of me wants to shout "Your beliefs are composed of piles of coprolites!" Part of me fantasizes vociferously arguing with my Southern relatives. I'd like to confront a childhood friend who still holds to beliefs he has championed since age thirteen. Even in my dreams, I return to the atavistic instincts and attack those who hold back human progress.

These old regressions to my animal heritage at times rather bother me. I know that such activity in real life is counter-productive. I have learned that when the ancestral aggression boils up in me, I must breathe, shake the thoughts out of my body and head, and immediately go over into my reasonable self. Internally, I visualize a ferocious tiger in a cage who occasionally sticks a paw with claws out through the steel bars and growls in a way that scares me.

Saying the last three paragraphs brings to mind some of more soft and tender readers who must be a bit shocked at my confession. I hope you do not relegate me to a 'Wild Man status'. I assure you that I have a strong conscious conscience lock on the cage. I have clear awareness of my aggressive animal instinct and have it fully under control. The above thoughts only run through my mind occasionally. As the old phrase of Transactional Analysis in the sixties had it "I'm OK and You're OK."

Taking Stock

My contention, and that of Evolutionary Psychologists, is that the thinkers among us must update all our theories about humans in the light of the natural instincts. EP theorists are quite explicit about how their new field is revolutionizing all social science disciplines which are not up to date on human science. I'll give one example from literature. Old biographies seek to capture a person's life still under the rubric of a unified mind as if their subject is a respectable human being. There is no awareness that a person has plural selves. For example, Walter Harrelson's recent book about Steve Jobs focuses on how Jobs was a rather driven irascible dictator. The resultant movie agrees with that depiction. Certainly, Steve Jobs did have parts which were anti-social, rather mean and callous, and unthoughtful. But, he also was an amazing innovator who introduced tremendously good options for humankind. Instinct theory in its broad range was not taken into account by Harrelson, and I think his resultant biography is slanted completely wrong because each of us is not homogenous unities; we contain multitudes.

But it is not just literary biographies that must be re-imaged with the new evolutionary information. Other social science disciplines are under the gun in terms of massive re-thinking. Disciplines that come to mind are anthropology, sociology, religion, psychology, and history – to name a few. We are in revolutionary times, academically speaking. The curriculums of universities are under attack by empirical evolutionary truths.

Universities need to re-think Darwin, evolution, and the power of instincts emphasized by Evolutionary Psychology and Liberation Psychotherapy. Both, pre-birth Nature and post-pregnancy Nurture are not in the least antagonistic. They both must be given their day in rational thinking about Human Nature.

By the way, isn't it interesting that it took a century and a half for Darwin's theories to be championed in the modern world? There was a lot of work by individuals who refused to get down in the mud with false fundamentalist theories and entrenched university politics which refused to allow the truth to come forth.

Neuroscience Additions

When I study modern neuroscience materials, I find myself completely fascinated. They too, are recognizing instincts remaining in the brain and are, more and more, studying emotions. For example, the work of Harry Harlow in the 1950's at the University of Wisconsin is now being given new consideration. Harlow's monkey research revealed that an infant chimp automatically wanted a soft cushiony mommy and would immediately - innately – know if the treatment of the mother was wrong. That rather colossal empirical finding has major import in terms of both knowing about early pathologies and even the field of ethics (because right and wrong happened to be wired in.)

I find that some of the sloppy thinking I have read in several Evolutionary Psychology texts is being empirically corrected by the careful scientific work of neuroscientists. I love this and plan to spend more study time in the field of neuroscience in the future.

Three Emotional Considerations

The work of Dr. Paul Ekman has been quite influential in emotional writings of Evolutionary Psychologists. Ekman's Darwinian scheme chose six emotions as did I, but there is a difference. He kept sadness, anger, scare, happiness and then, in his reading of <u>Emotions</u> gave credit to disgust and surprise. I did not find those two emotions significant in daily psychotherapy sessions though

I admit disgust was part of my mother's sibling rivalry Script. I see surprise as the forerunner of scare and do not treat it as a separate important category.

SASHET worked beautifully in therapy in thousands of situations as Dix and I could enter a person's hidden psychological depths by noting SASHET flashes, utilized SASHET in regression pursuits, and pointed to future fluidity by encouraging daily awareness of SASHET sensations in one's body.

Dr. Ekman consulted organizations and employees at transportation facilities. He taught seminar participants how to note his six emotions in their work so they could spot unhappy employees or even potential terrorists. My finding is that people frequently hide their emotions behind masks leftover from childhood or by being acceptable in society.

I have spent this time on Ekman because I believe Evolutionary Psychologists need to update their emotional lists. Surprise and disgust will not advance knowledge of Human Nature; excitement and tenderness will. There is much research done on sexuality. Can you imagine understanding sex without excitement and tenderness? Of course, you can visualize sexual encounters void of tenderness and excitement, but is that what you want?

A second emotional instinctual consideration has to do with the incest taboo. In the mid -1970s, a client named Zach showed up for a mandatory ten session contract with the hidden agenda of discovering whether I would be a good therapist for his wife whom he described as "highly neurotic". In about his sixth session Zach opened up and told how his mother had frequent psychotic episodes and his job as the oldest son was to deliver her to the Elgin State Mental Hospital for treatment. Upon one occasion when he was driving her to the hospital, she started ripping off her clothes and said "Please don't take me there. They give me rough shock treatment. If you take me back home I will be the sweetest f*** you will ever have. I'm good in bed; please take me home." Zack continued taking her to the hospital. When Zack told this story he broke up with massive sobbing. As therapist I noted how every member of the group tightened up when he quoted his mother. They were rather horrified by the scene with his mother.

In the same group was a Social Worker who had, as a child, been repeatedly raped by her biological father. Eustace was a good soul and a person who had fought through the old memories. She came to the place where she wanted to return to her home in the South in order to see if she could re-connect with family. When she returned to group a week or so later, Eustace reported that her father had, once more, roughly approached her as his sexual object. She was broken hearted. I stepped out of my usual role and became prescriptive: "Eustace, I do not think your biological father should any longer be considered as a legitimate Dad. I think it time to give up on him and find someone who will cherish your little girl within and provide solid soulful support." I repeat once again that I saw the group shudder with fear at the ugliness of her father.

These are two illustrations of the innate resistance to incest. To finish Eustace's story, I moved to a new location seventy miles away and no longer saw her in therapy. I did, however, see her again when I was having dinner at a restaurant in Chicago. She was laughing with friends, appeared so happy, and had her arm locked in the arm of a man who seemed to cherish her.

The third emotional clarification I must make has to do with terms that all too often are accepted in the therapeutic community: guilt, shame, depression, anxiety, and hatred.

Guilt is actually an inner dialog with two parts – one judgmental and rather angry and one part sad and repentant. Taking the guilt word apart and treating it as two parts in the mind proved immensely therapeutic.

Shame is used when a person visualizes an occasion when she/he has failed in terms of self-respect and, strangely, mind reads that others can see that old failed occasion and judge her accordingly. Again, de-constructing the shame word is very therapeutic.

All too often the word 'depression' is accepted as if the person is invaded by something like a virus. We saw that as making the person into a victim. We would ask "Which of the six emotions are you depressing?" When we got an answer, we led the person to keep letting that emotion out and not imploding it.

"Anxiety" is another 'it' word where a person thinks he or she is being invaded by an alien force. By keeping to the fluidity of the phrase 'scaring your-self' we made good progress in alleviating a person's pain. Clients learned to stop fantasizing negative futures and using full body breathing because panic occurs when the brain has insufficient oxygen.

Hatred is, of course, stacked occasions of anger, which we also took apart so a person could take charge of the internal fury.

Religion

The EP theorist Dr. Allen D. MacNeill gives four chapters of his Evolutionary Psychology textbook to the notion that there is a religious instinct. Other EP theorists go along with this idea also. I do not. Charles Darwin did not. I handle the notion of recurrent religion in quite another manner. I believe there are two causations for people going into religion and, for that matter, other ideological structures. The first is that all of us go through a three-to-five year old developmental stage where our brain/mind is drawn to magical, mystical, wish-filled imaginations. Even when we are grown, we still maintain that old developmental phase in our minds so we are drawn to Disney fantasies and Star Wars type struggles between good and evil.

I am convinced that the reflex back to the three-to-six fantasy period contributes to the interest in worshipping a god-like person who was apparently and supremely above the human condition. In addition, I know that there is a huge almost magnetic pull in our psychological being to return to options that offer the belonging dependency we experienced for so long... perhaps the first fourteen or so years. The long dependency of humans is fantasized in our unconscious minds as something wonderful and desirable.

Spelling this out quite plainly, the combination of the two elements in the last paragraph lead us to fall into the clutches of religious and secular ideologies which promise heaven on earth and beyond, a community family that embraces and cherishes us, and a thinking system which encompasses all the messy elements of life and provides a place of peace, love, and seeming absolute truth.

Unlike Evolutionary Psychology I am satisfied with this post birth understanding of religion. Like Darwin, I do not think there is any innate god-like pull installed in our mind/brains. Here is a case where people flee the seeming terror of aloneness and fall into the lap of thinking delusions and wish-filled illusions. Much better is accepting the solitude each of us is given and attaching ourselves to the miracles of nature and existence.

Clarification Concerning Therapy Sessions

In this writing I present the large (i.e. Meta) framework of a Twenty-First Century approach to psychotherapy. My goal has been to provide a larger picture - the context in which therapy can proceed. In actual live sessions with clients, we practiced and taught many paradigms drawn from other therapeutic systems.

We drew actual procedures to given problematic situations from Gestalt Therapy, Neuro-Linguistic Programming, Logo Therapy, Psychoanalysis, Client-Centered Therapy, Transactional Analysis, and a host of others, including Body Therapies.

Our idea was ever to use what really worked in regard to freeing a client's mind. To repeat, the evolutionary logic of this Monograph is to provide a foundation to a much larger superstructure. By listing the instincts, emotions, new under-standing of consciousness, and all the rest (like Presuppositions, Life Force Energy, Universal Abandonment fears, and the priority of SASHET), we provide clients with a mental grasp of the range of human nature. This proved to be quite freeing.

Chapter Three

The Modular Mind

So far we have established (with the help of Evolutionary Psychology) that the brain/mind is a collection of instinctual modules which dynamically influence human beings. The old Enlightenment belief that each of us is reasonable at the core has permeated education around the globe. Now we are in the process of updating social sciences which means, first of all, re-thinking education itself. This is no small task, and there will likely be enormous resistance by departmental fiefdoms in universities. So each alert reader must resort to an old evolutionary reflex – patience, which was necessary for hunters for hundreds of thousands of years.

I have added dynamic modules that are not part of the Evolutionary Psychology lexicon. (There will be resistance of those additions also.) I am absolutely insistent that big brain humans are not just innocent victims of instincts. I have studied two popular EP books recently: Dr. Robert Travers' The Folly of Fools and Dr. Robert Kurzban's Why Everyone (else) is a Hypocrite. Both books are firmly based on the central tenet of

Evolutionary Psychology, namely that modularity is a proven fact. However, what is not proven is that we need to be moralistically haughty and write books that are somewhat dismissive of those who still believe in noble Reason. I, for one, see no need to go to an opposite direction and proclaim that Reason is dead, though the homogenous unitary brain/mind is no longer valid. I will return to this in a later chapter.

A short review is in order. Yes, instincts are inherited, natural, and unlearned – meaning that they are not processed through our reasoning capacities. My contention is that, if our goal is to decipher all elements of basic Human Nature, we must consider adaptations which occur after the sheer biological imprints. Understanding the full range of motivation, perception, cognition, and behavior is at stake. I underscore what was said in the last paragraph: we humans are not just victims of our evolutionary instinctual heritage. The tragic reality is that there will be no final, balanced, definitive definition of Human Nature possible because of almost infinite combinations each human has. We can know the various elements such as instincts, emotional traumas, and the clean and warped six emotions, but to give a settled definition which brings total light on the human journey will probably elude us. Still, it must be attempted. Therefore, I now add dynamic processes which are quite active in human psychology.

Developmental Modules

1. Womb fixations occur due to sexual diseases, poor feeding, the intake of alcohol, and/or drug abuse by pregnant mothers. This means even before conception, some babies have marked traumas which, as said above, drastically effect motivation, perception, cognition, and behavior. (By the way, each of the following traumas creates difficulty with those four forces, but I shall not repeat them each time.) To understand the full breadth of potential psychological issues, therapists and even biological analysts, are wise to consider if there was actual damage done in utero. Indeed, there may be genetic complications. An example is in order. One mother asked me to work with her son in therapy. At the first session I discerned that he had physical mental issues due to his mother having consumed hard liquor when he was in the womb. To her dismay, I told her that therapy was not in order and made a rather strange recommendation. I suggested that he become a janitor at a fundamentalist Christian church where

he would be surrounded by true believers. Interestingly, he did become a janitor, joined the sect, learned their strict doctrines, and - womb ensconced in the faith's beliefs - made an acceptable life adjustment. While readers may have a choked clutch at my prescriptive solution, I watched the young man's adjustment for twenty years and he was rather happily okay. (Have you considered that the sanctuary of churches happens to be a substitute womb?) In addition, I think each of us has a remnant instinct that I label "the womb module." (Refer back to the Religion section in the last chapter.) Specifically, each of us has a latent desire for a safe, heavenly place where everything is taken care of.

2.   The first six months of life are quite important as all therapists know. Not only food, liquids, medicines and warm fuzzy mother attachment is at stake; so, too, is the importance of trust. Those who do not get this basic trust during the first six months become furtive in glances, distrustful of touch, and find themselves locked in what psychiatrists call 'paranoia' which is a mixture of anger and scare. I know of no 'one-plan-fits-all' solution to this primal kinesthetic deprivation. I do know that a caring female therapist is preferable to a male therapist because my wife Dix was very

effective for this early condition. Do we all have a module from this episode? The answer is in the affirmative though I stress that the module can be negative or positive. Do people ever pause to be grateful to a mother who was great at this level? Sadly, such gratitude speaking is seldom expressed. I do believe that my mother was superior in providing me a context that led to a basic happy trust in my organism.

3.   Next up, speaking developmentally, is the six to eighteen months stage which, once again, is vital in having a loving attaching mother. Here I think of several clients who later became rather obsessed with authenticity. One client, still wanting to be breast fed, would toss his glass baby bottles out on a hard floor where they broke and his mother, perforce, had to put him back on the breast. Another client despised a rubber pacifier and cried until he was in his mother's arms and next to her breasts. So, this is an important passage along life's way. If the stage is particularly thorny, the person – like my mother – develops a rather critical Projection syndrome and blames others for ordinary life difficulties. Does each of us have a remnant module from this developmental period? I declare "Yes!"

4. Then comes the two year old period where the child with a developing brain and beginning verbal consciousness seems to thrill in taking the opposite of parents. "Put on your shoes so you can go outside and play" says a father. "I don't want to wear shoes; I want to play barefoot" the child responds. "Okay" I said and let my son go play in the snow. Before long, he was back inside and wanted shoes. Dix says I was the best therapist for dealing with this issue, "Because you, Frank, have a major dose of 'taking the opposite!" I admit to being tickled inside when a client would have a "big dose" of the two year old module because I knew exactly what to do, therapeutically speaking. I noticed during my half century of doing therapy, college professors, CEO's, even high school teachers had large elements of this stage – evidenced by their listening marked by an almost eagerness to disagree, and frequent usage of "Yes, but." Does this developmental stage remain active in all of us? Yes. And the yes includes my sterling partner Dix, who has a teaspoon of this "Yes, but..." condition.

5. The three-to-six phase, as indicated earlier, is virtually loaded with magical thinking. A rather peculiar discovery of mine was that a person with a first six months problem would almost inevitably

use the four year old developmental phase as a major stopping place. They would major in fantasy, delight in spooky non-scientific thinking, and believe totally in the potions sold at Health Stores. These folks, twice stung in the first six years, were impervious to empirical facts. Rather, they rationalized that there was deep mystery in human affairs and delighted in the Wu-Wu books and thinking. One of the major therapeutic conditions which greatly resist normative therapy is when a mother psychologically 'marries' her son or a father psychologically 'marries' his daughter. Both child and parent resist therapeutic interjections which challenge their special relationship. The results of the unconscious marriage, however, are devastating. The parent who gives so much love to the child misses out on an intimate marriage. The child believes herself, or himself, always right resulting in all manner of pathological exhibitions. Tough though this stage may be, Dix and I were often successful when the child was willing to 'divorce' the parent. Of course, all of us have a small part that is also stuck at this stage, or why else would Hollywood keep making millions on fantasy films?

Beginning at about age three a child's brain has grown sufficiently so that he/she is figuring matters out in his immediate family. The child has realized that his/her body is separate, senses that something is wrong, figures that others (i.e. dad, mom, older sibling) have set patterns, and wants to feel more secure and safe. Therefore, with the brain power possessed, the child constructs what can be termed a personal philosophy wrapped in story form. The object of this interpretive structure is to provide predictability. This Script takes situations, events and significant people in the child's environment and places them in his safe narrative. The Script can be compared to a Broadway Play which has an antagonist, a protagonist, and actors and actresses adapting to life's conditions.

As days, weeks, months and years go by; the child rehearses the Play repeatedly. There is a STRONG, BUT HATED ROLE (The antagonist), the WEAK AND FEARED ROLE, and the ADAPTATION which provides a rather normal style of being. The Adapted role is fortified with a Defense Mechanism such as Denial (Nothing is wrong), Projection (You are wrong), Immobility

(Yawning passivity), Discounting (Yes, but), Conversion (Lightning means God is warning you), and more – all of which are fortified with rationalizations.

Again, the purpose of this inner narrative is to provide mental security across one's life. The roles are all known, the drama is set. We humans are storied creatures. Stories guide us and provide new insights into human affairs. Script, however, is a set narrative that knows no change and fights against re-consideration. The daily rehearsal across the years sets the drama into Mosaic stone carvings – the way to live and be. The pre-seven year old child, armed with a definitive story, can later place all people and all events within his previously decided upon narrative lines. Others encountered on life's path are simply shaped into the old roles (transference).

By now, you are (hopefully) grasping the power of this old narrative and the chains it can place on creativity, spontaneity, intimacy, daily awareness, and one's cognitive limitations. This secret bondage provides a 'cocoon' where new knowledge can easily go un-acknowledged. In fact, there is a barrier of resistance protecting the old story, a kind of Damocles Sword. This Sword threatens others, but also 'hangs over the head' of the sword waver. The fear is of vulnerable intimacy. The early child wanted to avoid, at all costs, the dependent vulnerability of the helpless infant. He or she takes charge and the Script goes on the stage platforms of life.

I repeat

Script is the major narrative underlying individual lives. In one of the previously mentioned developmental stages a trauma (or perceived trauma exaggerated by an age-appropriate thinking child) occurs, the child makes a philosophical decision (or premise), and then, daily, confirms that the decision is correct. I am finding this difficult to explain so I will refer back to my mother who, at about 20 months of age experienced her mother and father switch love energy (previously given to her), to Mildred - her newborn younger sister, As I have stated, this Script permeated my mother's identity and relationships. Not all the time, understand, but it was the largest and most destructive of all of her modules. Furthermore, the Script is unconscious (though quite dynamic and even dramatic in its negative causal results). No Script bound person is aware whatsoever of being initially programmed as a young child and, if a therapist points it out too early in therapy, the client will become effusive with denials.

Viewed in another manner, the Script often has three roles: victim, persecutor, and benign observer. A Script-bound person may say "You treat me as if I don't exist," "You are a drag," and then slip into a space where she/he simply looks upon the dreary scene of life with a sad child's eyes. My mother would complain about how my father treated her (the victim), then switch to attacking him as a "stupid hick" (the persecutor), and fall into a space where she was mentally absent to here-and-now life. A Script bound person plays out all three roles: Persecutor, Victim, and Innocent.

I could spend chapters providing illustrations of the huge negative effects of Script. I am flooded with memories of clients, especially trainees who would get into the Script module and – woof – be off in the stratosphere. It was a relief to me that it was not just my mother who was Script-bound, but each and every person I met, including myself and my wife. As a child I became obsessed with understanding Human Nature and my folks' pathology. Dix continually developed a module where she went into the future to discern possible problems in order to protect her scamp brother from getting into trouble with her father. At age eighty-one I am still lost in non-fiction study, and she still figures out what I am doing which might be problematic. These are scrap remnants of our old Scripts.

Therefore, I am not making the claim that anyone can ever become totally Script free. I believe that module will still exist, but with a difference. When therapy is taken seriously, the person will erase the negative personal and relationship problems, but will still have moments when that module can pop up. Picking on myself, I can get lost in play, observations of nature, greatly enjoy travel, but still have times when my head is in a book, and I do not want to be bothered, (or typing and do not want to be interrupted.) When Dix counsels me about some possible negative in my future, I heed her warning because she is very smart and perceptive, but I do not take the transference of being a Klutz brother.

The question is: Can the mighty unconscious Script be corralled? Yes. But it takes great concentration and usage of all the Big Brain's resources. The Sword's defense mechanisms must be consciously understood, un-armed by precise understanding of SASHET, and reactions slowed down until the Sword falls to the grave of the past. Accepting vulnerability is very scary. That is why Dix and I emphasize Tenderness.

Illustrations of Script

I smile. If you sat with me during a day's single sessions, couple sessions, and group therapy sessions, you would have no doubt about the destructive nature of Script. I will list a few of the old childhood situations which triggered a lifelong narrative: sibling rivalry, poverty, ignorance, verbal-physical-soul abuse, loneliness, bullying, alcoholic parents, step-parents, religiosity, privilege, boredom, parental stereotyping, parental death, specific traumas, and on we could go. Underneath a person's social personae, the unconscious Script grinds away. You will not see this on daytime dramas, but you can see this in the tragedies of Shakespeare or Sophocles. Novels sometimes show the underside of a person's character. The grand social parade on-line, the daily news, and other popular stories seek to place everything and everyone on the good-bad polarity.

A Script cannot be so easily categorized. It is simply an early creative narrative invented by a child. The unsolved Script, however, can be devastating and drastically limit a human's options, especially, intimacy.

Summation to this Point in this Book

My first point is that Evolutionary Psychology needs to expand its research beyond the instincts installed during the hunter-gatherer period of human evolvement. Otherwise, the use of the word "psychology" is entirely too limited. Human psychology is definitely marked by modules from the first six years. In addition, we are not just modular-driven robots. We do have mental capacities lower animals do not have. We are also the innovators who keep developing new options for humankind, said options which demand continual mental adjustments – like computers, televisions, mobile phones, automobiles, planes, etc. Furthermore, there is a plethora of stories, old and new, that are fallow in a person's makeup.

I had a fraction of a scare module because instinct theory and womb-upwards emotional theory are critical. And yet, we all live in a world where knowledge of instincts and the modules of

Liberation Psychotherapy are considered arcane to the max.

On July 10, 2016, 'Meet the Press' had four commentators talking about race in America. None of them expressed an awareness of the 'fear of strangers' instinct which we all have. None of the commentators seemed aware of SASHET feelings. I find this to be unacceptable ignorance which can lead to poor public policy.   We must get this knowledge out. Yes, only a few want to acknowledge being internally driven by eons-old instincts and pre-seven years of age thinking.

I am simply stating that the mental awareness of the rather vast array of instinctual influences and the tough-to-grasp insights of Liberation Psychotherapy will evade the great mass of people. And yet, I am convinced that this is the way of the future, a way which can truly liberate humans.

Chapter Four

Consciousness and the Unconscious

The Homo sapiens animal species' grasp of greater perceptive abilities and the growth of consciousness was one of the greatest breakthroughs in the 3.8 billion years of life and evolution. Several hundred thousand years ago one animal surpassed all other animals, and the robust story of conscious life started expanding. Surely, lower animals have levels of consciousness in that they protect their offspring, register pain and pleasure, are primitively aware of their environment, and follow instincts like building nests. The erect biped Homo sapiens, however, remembers the past and can mentally project into the future, and is able to communicate complex phenomena, develop abstract languages, and create new tools. Over time brain development kept continuing and consciousness kept expanding as culture grew.

In the modern world consciousness is both a blessing and a bane. The blessing is the advanced intelligent awareness all of us possess, and the bane is that we are basically unaware of how the brain/mind works in terms of innate instincts which motivate us, unconsciously, in irrational directions. The conscious rational mind is superb and has led us to almost unimaginable scientific conquests. Taking just one, the immediate ability to access the world's information in seconds via the Internet happens to be a colossal achievement.

And yet, unconscious instincts drive us to the edge of destruction with atomic and hydrogen warfare, global warming denial, chemical and biological weapons – each of which could lead humanity to ultimate ruin. Here, communication has fallen apart. Before Darwin and Evolutionary Psychology, there was no real recognition that we – the intelligent species – happen to have inner drives which are the same as animals roaming the jungles and savannahs many thousands of years ago.

We have ideologies the world over which are scant more than the mumblings of orangutans, but the motivations driving them are scant under-stood. "Scant understood" until Evolutionary Psychology began to resurrect the thinking of Darwin so magnificently written about in <u>The Origin of the Species</u>, <u>The Descent of Man</u>, and <u>The Expression of Emotions in Men and Animals</u>.

To Evolutionary Psychology I have added the contribution of Liberation Psychotherapy which begins and ends with six - rarely taken into consideration - emotions.

The Cloud

Consciousness is like a narcissistic cloud that confuses the grand mass of humans with the erroneous belief that they have perfectly logical singular rational minds. This monograph has shown that belief to be a terrible delusion, said delusion with its thousands of irrational ideologies, seriously threatening life on this earth. Is there a way out? Evolutionary Psychologists are beating the drums in universities, seeking to awaken the old social science paradigms, with the bold truth of our unconscious instincts which, unchecked and without awareness, are hurtling humanity to a bad end.

Here I stress a truth all too often overlooked. When consciousness came forth in human brains and minds several hundred thousand years ago, it is understandable – nay 'necessary' – that there was no awareness of internal driving instincts. Rather, the emerging humans had to focus on surviving and surviving meant using all one's mental functions to figure out how to store food, kill food, select non-poisonous plants, make medicines, develop villages, and do everything possible to pass on their genes to the next generation. People may have had a faint awareness of, like me, the tiger within, the appearance of one's own greed and acquisitiveness, or even community building with empathy and cooperation, but first of all, they had to survive. And survival meant using every bit of their logical minds.

How is consciousness narcissistic? Well, people – from age two on – want desperately to believe that they are rational, right, reasoned, well-balanced, and logical. Adults and children alike do not want to hear that they are wrong, misguided, or making a big mistake. They won't hear of it. Each person, above all, believes himself possessing a unified mind. No question about it. All the Mechanisms of Defense come to bear when there is the slightest suggestion from others that they are in error. It is not only therapists who know this; it is also parents, teachers, trainers, managers and anyone seeking to pass on human information. Taking in technical information is different. When it comes to someone's personality, however, the grand barrier reef of narcissism is thick, wide and high.

BB-8

In the Star Wars movie "The Force Awakens" a new mechanical creature is introduced. **BB-8** is a droid robot shaped like a volley ball, but with a difference. Perched on the top is what can be described as a round mobile phone brain device about two inches thick. The eight panels of the 'volley ball' gather information and send the data to the 'head' control center. Now, here is the thing: as the main ball rolls around gathering information, the decision-maker head stays vertically on top of the ball!

In my thinking, this is the perfect image of consciousness, which, when we are vertical (and not horizontally asleep), gathers disparate information from all manner of sensors, all manner of pure animal instincts, and all manner of psychological modules. The control 'head' is totally unaware of the varying sources, speaks and thinks as if there is no variation and it is perfectly cohesive and unified, and acts and makes decisions accordingly. *I stress that our brain/minds are totally unaware of multiple intake channels.* (I add the cautionary advice that it is best not to make major decisions when getting input from the Script channel.)

What better image of consciousness could be imagined? I know not. In this case, fiction is better than straight true logical explanation. I laughingly add....**We all have BB-8 brains!** Consciousness is simply that way.

Academic Resistance

Consciousness with its delusional belief in a homogenous mind is enormously thick (headed). Just the other day I read of a study of college professors who were to rank how their teaching did in comparison to members of their department. Each Prof placed himself in the top twenty per cent; none graded themselves lower. This Consciousness veil of narcissism descends when it comes to the subject of this Monograph. To say to a history professor that his analysis of key figures throughout the decades and centuries is off base because it does not know mental multiplicity, is to court academic-sounding wrath. To suggest to an educational department that they need to incorporate evolutionary insights into their teaching – both in students and material – is to engender rebellion. Old, settled humanitarian pathways will not allow their profession to go in different directions. I am underscoring how consciousness itself is the hidden issue.

Consciousness is the grand protector of human irrationality, the protector of harmful ideologies, and the Grand Inquisitor who uses words to avoid truth, especially unwanted unconscious truth. Who, in deed, wants to admit that their intellectual venture has been built upon faulty ground? Who wants to think that he is not the master in his own skull? Who has the courage to begin all over again in the attempt to understand Human Nature? Damn few. I guarantee it.

As Time Passed in Human History

Part of expanding consciousness is asking one's self, *"Who Am I?"* I will most certainly die, so, *"What is worth doing in the meantime?"* I live among other people, so *"How shall I treat them and they treat me?* These questions must have reverberated throughout history and we all know that the three questions have permeated the religions of the world. With the final arrival of knowing about instincts and emotions, we have superb clues at both deciphering human dysfunction and figuring out new ways for education – beginning with parenting and extending through Foreign Policy and Global Policy. This is a great opportunity!

A Metaphor

Knowing both the modules of Evolutionary Psychology and the additional modules of Liberation Psychotherapy, we can conceive of a human as a piano with 88 keys. Since we grasp how consciousness seals off a great deal of instinctual and emotional awareness, how can we relate in an entirely new way? Wise readers that you are, you know that the answer has to do with how we choose the keys, what pressure we put in the tips of our fingers, and how we use the foot petals to make good or wonderful music. Bluntly, we can, as one of my books has it, *"Tell people who they are"*. Presuppositions are the mode.

One of our trainees was a teacher in a rough urban district where crime was at a high rate throughout the community. Jean reveled in the power of one of our subjects: Presuppositions. We explained the many ways a person could use language influentially in terms of identity and relationships. She became expert in the subject. She realized that her main task was not teaching just reading, writing and arithmetic. Her main job was to build character. Jean told our group about one of the young men in her class who was daily irritating and tried to set her up to give him the same treatment he received at home: utter rejection. This boy, Leroy, was on his way to becoming a bully, a terrible student, and a budding anti-social criminal.

Jean said to him sentences like the following: "Leroy, you are not being yourself today. What's going on?" Leroy would shake his head with confusion because, consciously speaking, he was following in his father's model and being problematic. "Come now, Leroy, I don't buy you not knowing this lesson for a second; I know you have a good brain so don't try and fool me." When he showed a moment of bullying, Jean would say "Get back to being your real self and quit messing around." In other words, she bombarded this boy with presuppositions about his worth, his thinking abilities, and what he really wanted in life. After chiding him the day before about not being himself due to one minor slip, Leroy came in the next day and said, "Miss Jean, I am back to being the real me today."

Yes, that is a simple illustration. But, it is a telling one. Since people do not really know who they are inside, smart teachers, excellent leaders, and adequate therapists can tell people who they are. I am insisting that Jean's maneuver in one situation can provide a model for all our transactions.

Mental multiplicity understandings of the unconscious provide each astute person a golden opportunity to shape people into their best options. We may see an old instinct of aggression in someone, but we need not buy it as the reality. Since each liberated intellectual wants to pass on the available truths in his/her particular profession, the method of information distribution must add on the ability to change each person's character – to their openness to truth.

Wow!

Here someone may well think the unconscious teaching of which I am speaking is naught other than positive cheerleading. Nothing could be further from the truth, nothing! I am introducing a new art form: **People Creation**. If you were a wise person from a distant planet of a distant galaxy, *not possible of course because of the speed of light*, you would note that humans are always in the process of shaping others. We do this by asking questions leading to answers out of our own primitive philosophy, and behavior. We may not be conscious of our shaping others, but the reality is that we do it with each shrug, word and interpretation. For the astute, learning the Presupposition Mode of Teaching there are three considerations if one wants to take charge of unconscious guiding to their best selves: Philosophical, Behavioral, and Verbal.

Adjustments for Consciousness and Unconsciousness

My quick take on consciousness and unconscious shaping in this monograph, is far less than I would prefer. In our Training Groups we taught Presuppositions for six months at three day sessions. Therefore, I am displeased with such a short treatment of such a major subject. I will return to this in the final chapter because, if your goal is to be effective with people, presuppositions offer the best path.

I glory in consciousness, but grieve at how consciousness itself provides a narcissistic barrier which is difficult to pierce. It is a cloud – a dark cloud hiding the sun. If any reader simply wants to deny the reality of the effect of un-realized dynamic power of instincts (including emotions) the above considerations must be obtuse at best. These words would be mere gobbledygook. But, for those who have followed the material of the preceding chapters and have watched helplessly, as instincts have driven their friends, and created havoc in their families, this information about a process which really works (Presuppositions) must be welcomed with open arms.

The Presuppositional Process

Three Steps:

1) Decide upon your desired outcome.
2) Speak your presupposition as if the outcome is real here and now. No question about it.
3) Having spoken the 'reality', you never retreat one iota. You spoke the real truth, and that is it. (*Think of the teacher, Jean, and the student, Leroy...*)

Presuppositions provide the means to manage modularity.

Chapter Five

Natural Morality and Ethics

My Caged Tiger Growls

There is more nonsense written about morality in human history than all subjects added together. Let's just take the phrase *Imago Dei* – the idea that you are born in the image of God and should, yes **should,** straighten up and fly right! Or else! Do not disappoint God!

Excuse me! What cloistered cleric came up with that one? Not only is the thought cloudy and indecipherable, we are to "clothe ourselves in righteousness" because of some weird image that any person can twist any way he or she wants. The Tiger growls: "We are animals, people! We inherit animal instincts, some of which can lead to genuine morality and some of which can leave us greedy competitors, red in tooth and claw while being lost in the narcissistic mire of self-interest. Wake up! Re-think! There is a path to true morality following the hints which evolution itself provides."

Notes from Previous Lesson

Instincts that can lead to true natural morality and daily ethics are empathy, cooperation, family love, tribal loyalty, and even play, creativity, and curiosity. But, since we are the animal with the Big Brain and can think and make decisions, each of the above listed instincts can be twisted with the golden strand of narcissism or wed with other instincts which can only lead to human dysfunction. Reasonable people must use their wisdom to choose to emphasize the seven listed instincts in this paragraph's first sentence. Sadly, reason does not always win out, so I move to a second category.

We learned that babies reveal six emotions. They have sad cries, angry cries, and scared reactions, are basically happy, kick their legs with excitement, and are tender loving little creatures. (Every parent treasures those curious moments when an infant reaches up and touches your face with absolute trust.) *Philosophically considering those SASHET emotions in their infantile exhibitions, we **note** that each of them has a* *quality reference.* In plain language, each emotion signals a good or bad, a right or wrong, a healthy expression or a pathological one. This means that we are introduced by natural emotional reactions to morality (which is the overall system of right/wrong and good/bad) as well as ethics (which is the system of daily exchange also on a good or bad basis.) Furthermore, we could put all the baby emotional reactions on a pain/pleasure continuum and, by so doing, expand our understanding of both morality and ethics.

A third consideration came forth from infant observation when I noted they have primitive awareness of beauty, truth, justice, goodness, and love. Let us explore those primal values.

Beauty: Babies are fascinated and curious about colored baubles, and explore with their fingers to see if something is soft and cuddly or hard, cold and rough. Later, we cultured adults extend those early looks, sounds, and gestures into thousands upon thousands of beautiful-to-the-eye manifestations, love the full range of music, and prefer silk to burlap.

Truth: A newborn anticipates a soft mother (as Harlow learned from chimps – and I learned from my children), and – if there is the opposite, the newborn feels cheated. Authenticity of skin encounters, authenticity of care, authenticity of sound, and authenticity of the entire safe structure of sleeping conditions is not optional; a baby demands those. They are optional for survival, but I can assure you, my half century of therapy experience informs me that the four authentic demands of infants – if ignored or denied – leads to an unhealthy adult. Earlier I also gave several illustrations of a child's reaction when weaned too early. I add up all these factors and conclude that a child is showing early signs of the demand for truth. Honest treatment from providers is expected. Anything less is an invitation to pathological chaos.

Justice is similar to truth in that an infant's demand for fairness later builds up into the world of law and societal everyday cooperation. Note that I am referring to small, but significant, signs seen in a baby's crib or in the arms of a loving parent. Basic fairness is as far as many present-day adult's thinking extends. They think that is justice. For instance, allowing minorities to enter college on a quota basis seems 'unfair' and many protest. Justice, however, takes into account history (ex. Several hundred years of slavery) and seeks to balance matters out. Our Big Brains, joined with empathy and social survival, means a <u>just re-balancing</u> must be accomplished.

I risk being repetitive when I arrive at the value of Goodness. Goodness, in my lexicon, means kindness, neighborly care, reaching out personally and volunteering at food banks, collecting clothes for indigents, and providing shelter like Habitat for Humanity. I contend that goodness starts right there at a baby's crib when a mother or father considers the infant's welfare is first on the agenda – that is if we want a healthy adult. As stated before, babies are not passive, patient creatures. They expect good care and, if it is not forthcoming, will install a trauma which means later personal and relationship trouble.

Love... Now I *know* that I am being repetitive. Still, the foundation of being a tender loving adult is poured (like concrete) right there at the foot of a baby bed. Babies know what they want and that involves dozens of daily ministrations. It is true that a person can decide, later, to forego tender intimate relationships, and I saw that hundreds of times. Anyone, who has held a tender dependent infant looking up into your eyes with ultimate trust, develops one mental module that knows what is really valuable. And, also the adult knows that unless you treat a partner in the same cherishing manner you treat a vulnerable infant, you will not find true intimate love.

But, wait a minute! *Love* had thousands of meanings, iterations, and expressions. By emphasizing the baby-parent form, I intend to show the psychological stance for all loving expressions – like love of Nature's magnificent panoply, like love of humankind, like appreciate of one's body which has miraculous functions (like the immune system), and sheer love for being a part of the human experience for all too short of a time. Remember, we are talking about natural foundations for morality

A Different Slant

I rather sneaked one source in earlier, namely the stance taken by a loving father or mother. Nothing can replace those years. Nothing! A parent's natural treatment of a dependent baby provides a model of the basic moral stance as well as daily ethics. When you embrace everything written about in the first four chapters, you will realize that each person is a collection of major parts, among which are natural instincts, psychological childlike remnants, later developmental remnants, and adult remnants. My point is that morality begins when we cherish the little child in whomever we encounter. (And let me tell you that I could tell client stories at this point until you cried for relief – "Enough Frank! Enough!")

There is a grand grace to being a parent and hearing your child learn and say the word "mommy" or "daddy" – the best two words in language. Plus you get the privilege of watching them grow, having them go through skinned knees due to too much expression of excitement, watch them learn in school, and on and on. Though a parent feels sad when it becomes necessary for a child to separate and tells you forcefully to back off, that, too, is good. I actually felt happy when my kids put me in my place because I knew it was a necessary step to identity.

Morality? Ethics?

If someone asks "What does this have to do with morality and ethics?" my answer is that raising a child goes both ways: we take care of them and they teach us what is valuable and important. Just by having the hallowed responsibility/opportunity of being a protective parent we, who are swaddled in love daily, are learning morality. Every person we encounter was once a mother's precious baby. When I read that, in war situations, the killing of another human being is core shocking, I think soldiers are being forced to wake up to the truth that they have just killed a mother's child. Natural morality begins at the point when each of us realizes that life, which is shot through with complexity, turns out to be quite simple when we add things up as has been explained by all previous paragraphs: morality is about love.

Again, I hear a demurring voice that says: "Frank, stop the mushy stuff. Morality sometimes means protecting the tribe, the community, the nation and that may well mean war and killing. I have no defense. My critic is right. Remember that I saw soldiers from World War II, Korea, Vietnam, Iraq and Afghanistan. They experienced what the polite rest of us have not, nor should we ever, experience. I loved the men I worked with who courageously stood up under horrible conditions. I have no moralistic judgment in me. I understand Post Traumatic Stress Disorder.

In fact, the greatest compliment I ever received was from a Vietnam vet who was often in "the bush" meaning that he was out in the jungle fighting. He carried a 50 caliber automatic weapon and told me of his squad being chased through the jungle by large numbers of Viet Cong. My client's job was to bring up the rear and spray the jungle behind his friends. "I would hear the Viet Cong sandals padding on the dirt and would turn and let them have it. Then, I would run like hell." At one point this guy was railing about citizens who "have no damn idea what it is like to have crazies shooting at you and running for your life." Then, he paused and said "Frank, I would have been glad to have you by my side in the bush because you would be there a hundred per cent." I feel tender tears as I remember that comment.

Continuing now, I assure readers that morality does not mean simplistic saccharine thinking. Complexity rules. I know that pathology provides erratic gene combinations, poor womb treatment, failures in attachment, and so on. I know that some parents provide terrible models for their children. I have seen much pathology across the years. (Human pathology was – in effect – my time in "the bush.") Nothing I say about the beauty of babies or the wonder of parenthood as a natural foundation for morality and ethics is to diminish the complexity we all must deal with – soldiers especially. Life does not provide simple answers.

Society, Culture and Educational Input

In whatever community any of us traveled during our first eighteen or so years on our journeys to adulthood, there were unspoken assumptions as to acceptable behavior. As the popular saying has it, "It takes a village to raise a child." I believe that. I muse back to my years in a neighborhood in Memphis, Tennessee. In those days, neighbors were always watching and, if you did something nutty, they would call your parents. That is not done anymore, but anywhere kids grow up there is a kind of cocoon of care evidenced with Band-Aids, warnings, and respectable models. A growing child hears music, notes how homes are decorated and lawns taken care of, as well as noting stained glass in churches and how fruits and vegetables are arranged in stores. Schools have educational materials in their libraries, teachers who do their best to get you to the next level, and lessons which tell the difference between right and wrong. Laughingly I say, "It takes a lot of work to have bad morality and convince others through negative signals to lead them into negative branding generalizations such as: "That kid is just no good." "Leroy is worthless."

Once Presuppositions and Modularity are mastered, such abominable black and white moralizing is eradicated.

A Bible phrase comes to mind: "We are surrounded with a great cloud of witnesses." Philosophically, it must be noted that every child *selects* among the various phenomena surrounding them, *emphasizes* whatever they will to form their opinion, and *interprets* all the human interactions in whatever way he or she so chooses. Presuppositions can give the needed nudge so individuals can have a moral self-image.

Summation

Inter-connected globalization, the host of massive humanity destructive weapons, the close connection of everyone in the world through cell phones-computers-social web sites, and mass migrations due to war and climate change, all lead to one conclusion: we must get along. We must shed, for instance, the instinctual stranger fear, the conscious reflex to narcissism, and raw self-interest Capitalism. We must embrace human brotherhood. The survival of the Homo sapiens species must be based on how seriously we want to emphasize the first primary instinct – to stay alive. This basic Life Force Instinct cannot be trumped by resorting to racism, sexism, or nationalism. As a species, we must awaken to our innate instincts and our natural emotions as this monograph spells out. Solidarity with all of humanity is definitely revealed in our evolutionary heritage which has taken us from bacteria of billions of years ago to erect animals. The last six million years have evidenced a Big Brained animal walking on the face of the earth who, most recently, has manufactured instruments of destruction along with instruments of technological togetherness. There is a universal Human Nature. There are natural paths to humanity embracing morality and daily ethics.

We must accept what Nature has given us, put all our instincts in perspective, and balance everything with our marvelous brains which can think matters through and make life-giving decisions.

Chapter Six

The Meaning of Psychological Liberation

In 1974 I taught an evening psychology class at Wright Junior College in Skokie, Illinois. At the first session I asked class members (mostly males in their forties) what they wanted from the course. I took notes. One intelligent businessman who was quite successful said "I come from a family of high achievers. I have a young son, who is very retarded, and I am ashamed of him, and I don't want to be." (*Notice the differing 'I' parts which this man exhibited in a short time.*)

I gave him an assignment: "At each one of our sessions I want you to report on some life lessons your son taught you during the past week." His reports became the highlight of the course. "This week I joined with my son and watched ants taking crumbs to their underground nest." "We played with little balls on the floor; he was teaching me to, once again, notice colors and shapes." "We touched things this week – he likes soft objects, the feel of a flower, and the touch of my hand." Sometimes the reports were given with tears, and I assure you were poignant and very instructive to all of us. His last report went something like this: "My son taught me to appreciate small things, to laugh, and to play: I had forgotten all of those." The class applauded him.

Stages along the Journey

I suggest that the first liberation lesson is the mere acceptance of the simple objects of beauty, the acceptance of the joyful child inherent in all people, and the willingness to cherish our own souls.

How do we get there? It seems that the first step is quelling the narcissism that automatically comes with consciousness. We must "get down on the floor" and examine how our lives are programmed by instincts. We must make sure we exercise our minds beyond just the array of ancient evolutionary tendencies. We must go through our blocked emotions, and re-think old value obsessions begun before age seven.

We must ask, "Who did I copy and how do I put that old program into place so I walk around in someone else's skin part of the time?" "Do I manipulate others with phony emotions to be liked?" "Do I still display one of the six basic emotions to keep others away?" "What old decisions begun by a little child still motivate me in my adult life?" "How can I be aware of SASHET feelings and be real, have peacefulness in my soul, and laugh, play and appreciate small things?"

Not easy. None of those questions have simple answers, and none are won without soul sweat or serious self-examination. Is that worth it? Only a given reader can answer that. My job, in this chapter, is to spell out steps along the Liberation Trail. My clients (or at least most of them) were willing to struggle through the swamp of conscious narcissism in order to gain the reward of being authentic, knowing what they wanted down deep, and building their lives around beauty, truth, justice, goodness and love.

To Examine or Not Examine: That is the Question.

Is the unexamined life not worth living as Socrates said? The old philosopher was making too harsh a generalization. We all live with unacknowledged and unknown drivers from childhood remnants and none of us will be perfect – no matter how much self-examination we do. Even the great foe of Script may contain positive elements – like my drive to figure out psychological solutions for others, like another's passion to make money, or still another's impetus to be the smartest woman in the room.

No one will end up perfect. We all make some compromises just in order to survive both in life and marriage. I have often said that intimacy is "a bonus" and not necessary whatsoever to have a good peaceful life. Still, there is an incessant insistent Child within who demands that each of us gets the most out of life that we have before our certain end. That entails honing our minds with the best information possible, expanding our awareness by perceiving more clearly, and making our souls larger and larger with the multiple meanings of love. This un-tiring Inner Child pushes us to get what we really want, do what we think fulfilling, and honestly feel our way through the vicissitudes of life.

Dysfunction Review

Some follow the raw animal instincts provided for us by a large number of animals across the eons. I have flashes of people encountered across the years who are stuck at this level: criminals who lie, cheat, steal, and even murder just in order to gain moments of feeling sated – like a lion eating his prey; addicts who gain mental peace for a while, as they, in the process, destroy their bodies; and society's users who use their intelligence to con others out of their resources. These people who live in the swamp of narcissism have whiffs of liberation, but they never get the real reward.

Immediately though, I want to add that each of us must come to terms with our animal instincts. Approaching marriage as license to be wildly sexual without true tenderness is not a lasting good option. Defining yourself as a bully in business provides a lonely journey. Thinking life is about acquisitions and adding numbers to your financial holdings is a rather boring mathematical delusion.

We must go through the list of animal instincts and cull out those who might well steal our souls while providing a dismal walk to nowhere. We must 'cage" those innate drives which do not lead to having a liberated soul – a person lost in gratitude for life's phenomenal gifts.

Then, there is Script, my devilish opponent throughout all my years of doing therapy. Here the grand knowledge of how consciousness fools us like **BB-8**, is of tremendous importance. Once we know the absolute reality that each of us is not a unique, single-minded, coherent entity, we are well on the road to psychological freedom. Why? Because humility and openness are the only ways out of the maze! No longer can anyone live under the delusion of saying, "I'm me and that's that. I'm good and know who I am and what I am doing!" When the multiple mind and its multiple sources are understood to be pasted together under the veil of consciousness, reality itself must be faced. None of us has it 'all together'; none of us is a single mental unity; all of us have many modules; we all have multitudes within.

The toughest **BB-8** challenge is to take on one's Script – that neuronal pathway forged since a young child. We know that, as the **BB-8** sphere rolls along, there will be automatic responses programmed from yesteryear. The challenge is to take charge of consciousness and choose to put your best self forward – not a repetition of the old junk. I, the writer of this monograph, know this to be quite difficult; but I also know those who have accomplished it.

Along the way, **BB-8** will roll through many old memories and traumas which were acting-out points of the old Script. My experience tells me that the way out is through and 'through' means feeling the blocked emotion, making appropriate sounds, and full breathing as the old repressed stuff is allowed out of your organism. This, too, is hard to accomplish alone without another there to hold your hand, but it is doable: breath, move, feel, and make full noise to let it all go.

Old pathological invitations, seen rightly, are a tremendous invitation to grow. Excitement follows the knowledge of our having a lot of old modules, a superb challenge to take charge and use the full resources of the Big Brain, and fight our way to liberation. To know that each of us has multiple minds is to lead the wise to, perhaps, the greatest sign of true liberation – the way of Presuppositions.

The Transformative Power of Presuppositions

We know that each of our brain/minds is like a collage. Know also that each person we meet also possesses a "multitude" in their heads. Furthermore, they are somewhat confused when they sense the mental multiplicity because they do not even understand themselves. This means that a tremendous opportunity awaits the wise. *We can tell them who they are.* The idea is to build freeing self-images.

First, we must ward off their conscious verbal forays where they think their mental constructions are right, true, honest, and real. They will have no awareness of their frequent switches with the "I word". They will remain serious when discussing this or that and will not know that an astute observer/listener can hear flashes of childlike thinking, childlike reasoning, childhood wishing, and moments of the speaker's being totally lost in Script as he or she continues the old narrative. Thus, our first step is noting the switches and not being deluded with the conscious formulations. After all, the astute can note the changes of voice, the mannerisms which show differing personae, and the content which goes all over the place.

Second, recognizing the "88 keys of the piano" as they are randomly struck, the one who knows presuppositions has a wonderful path to meaningful dialog. Go back to the first paragraph of this chapter and note how I took the last "I" of the businessman and played on that "key." I went with where his tender emotion was. My assignment was designed for this terrific guy to get more in touch with what is finally valuable: Learning to love with utter simplicity.

My contention is that each dialog with another can be simple intellectual exchanges or liberating exchanges. (This is especially true in intimate loving relationships.) We can hit the keys on the piano in any way we desire. If we want chaos and disagreement, we pound away with rational talk and will get the result of negativity. But, if we begin to learn the power of presuppositions, we become the greatest artists of all: the creators of human potential. Remember: the person has not only all the pathology available; he/she also has all the creative potential available.

Lessons in Presuppositions

The idea is to bring out the best in others. I often think how a great comedian can bring out laughter and joy in an audience by her/his words, behavioral style, and little gestures like a wink, a hand wave, a shift of eyes, and a lilt to the voice. That is an example of how the comedian has **assumed** a reality and has set up all delivery to get the anticipated result. First, we piano players must get the initial assumption/presupposition clearly in mind. If you want your spouse to be more loving, you assume that he/she wants the same thing, is eager to touch and cuddle, and wants to be soul close. If you assume that he is a boring drudge, you will get a boring drudge. (Others read our assumptions and play them out!)

Therefore, the **first step in the Presuppositional Process** is to have a clear outcome in mind.

The **second step** is to get your goal firmly in mind and act/say *as if* the goal already exists in the here-and-now. Not in the future. Not railing about something in the past. Your goal already exists and you are simply noting it and underscoring it. Decide on your desired outcome upfront.

The **third step** is you never go back on what you have said is true. The reality exists, period. End of appraisal. Think of the good teacher mentioned earlier. She knew Leroy had what it takes to understand and learn and she would never retreat one iota. If Leroy did anything to the contrary of her basic assumption it was either her fault as a teacher or he was, "Not being himself today." Therefore, the point is that truth delivered is never compromised by other transactions.

Three Forms of Presuppositions

I figured out 26 different linguistic forms which can be used to provide variety in installing new self-concepts in others. One category is Authority

Presuppositions where, you, the speaker, deliver your desired outcome as if you are a Pope, President, CEO, Principal, and the Ultimate Leader speaking the Ultimate Truth. For example, I taught a trio of simple statements: "You are," "You have," and "You will." "You are excellent students to stick with me as I list a number of linguistic phrases." "In my estimation, you have what it takes to do well in life – and, I suppose, you got this drive from one of your grandparents." "You will always choose the best in life because I know you want a good life."

There are other forms of Authority Presuppositions which you may read about in my book, Tell 'Em Who They Are, available from Amazon .com.

A rather quaint category begins with the word 'what.' "What strikes me about your educational drive is that you will learn whatever and wherever you are." "What is important at this point is that you learn from your mistakes because people like you and me are always growing." "What is perfectly wonderful is your good attitude which you will have all your life and will take you through any difficulty that will come along."

Linguists have a category called 'Factives', which means a word assumes a reality. Consider the question "Are you aware that you are an intelligent person?" "The word 'aware' is a Factive. Other Factives are 'know', 'realize', 'learn', 'are cognizant of', and 'call to your attention'. Each of those phrases can be used in the 'intelligent person' sentence. Our trainees loved Factives and almost got stuck in using this category because it was so effective.

The Captivating Wonder of Presuppositions

When I start talking about this subject, I am flooded with happiness due to all the transformations I have seen across the decades with this particular topic. Once a person adheres to taking up the presupposition style of being, several things change. One, the person takes a massive step away from narcissism because you are thinking about others, not yourself. Two, a person who knows the modular mind has a great advantage in presupposition work because he/she knows what buttons to push. Three, it is rather shocking to see how magically presuppositions work. (I could go off on this one for hours because both Dix and I saw the effect of presuppositions daily, plus we received reports back from our students – reports of rather astounding results.)

Just think of the power of this subject in terms of parenting, grandparenting, teaching, leading, speaking, and family encounters – to mention a few. This chapter is about Liberation. Those who decide to have presuppositions take over their interchanges with others, find a new joy within. They have found a mission in life quite unlike any of the old adages of religion which also offered a loving style – but without the information of how, precisely, to be a redemptive person.

Excitement is expressed with another category I termed Enthusiasm Adjectives. Some of the people I trained used this category incorrectly as they would say things like "You are great, you are super, you are terrific" which, though they have the "You are/ have/ will" phrase in them, *are definitely not the best use of Enthusiasm Adjectives.* Patiently, I would teach that the idea is to give the targeted person a **personality quality** which sinks in. Therefore: "I think it super how you are continually learning," "I am inspired at how your curiosity is just great." "Your terrific drive to learn about science makes my heart feel good."

Two Caveats

The first caution is to know the Script Child was seeking to figure out a life path which guaranteed survival and deserves respect. Therapeutically speaking, the goal is to re-route Life Force energy – not to eradicate it. With inner dialogues the therapist discovers the original positive intent of the client. The next step is to point the Inner Child to a more beneficial path.

The second caution is to underscore that Liberation Psychotherapy is not a set fundamentalist system impervious to new truths. Though we trained three hundred students in Lib Psych, we do not have a cadre of true-believer therapists. We always insisted that trainees keep growing and be open to new helpful information. I admit that Liberation Psychotherapy is time-bound and incomplete. Personally speaking, Dix and I continually stressed our ideas to be fluid, dynamic and open. Keep learning!

Summary

I am confident that liberation means far more than I have explained in this chapter. I found myself, during the course of this writing, having flashbacks to my class at Wright Junior College back in the seventies. The reports of the businessman were captivating to all of us in the classroom. My flashbacks indicate a sense of those old startling revelations actually providing a metaphor for all of us.

Each of us, as it turns out, has a developmentally challenged Child within – a part of us who wants to be cherished and not shunned, a beautiful little girl or boy who wants to be loved by a parent, *i.e. the grown-up reading this monograph.*

**Each of us has a task
to bring this little child to consciousness
in order to discover the beauty of simplicity,
the wonder of appreciation,
and the glory of love.**

EPILOG

An old story has it that Beethoven's servant told his master he was resigning. Beethoven was both shocked and incensed: "You can't resign! You are my inspiration!"

The servant laughed...and said: "Let me see... I am YOUR Inspiration!" Then he sang: "Ha, ha, ha, hah" to the following notes.

Beethoven later began his Symphony #5 with those musical notes.

Do you experience questions about Life? We are all servants and each of us contributes. Remember Beethoven's opening bars of Symphony #5!

Please remember that symphonies are sometimes structured by introducing a theme, having that theme peek out during the course of the work, and a Finale where the theme is marvelously concluded.

The analogy with Liberation Psychotherapy holds. The original theme presents a strong request that students forge beyond conscious awareness and begin to learn **SASHET** – *Sad, Angry, Scared, Happy, Excited and Tender*. Those six emotions provide an entry point to vital self-knowledge.

The SASHET symphony continues as a person learns to capture the false displays of emotions consisting of copies, manipulations, and old traumatic emotional assemblages. The latter are released through full breathing, bodily expression, and the beginning sounds of freedom. The Liberation Symphony is now underway.

Then the Finale, as Tenderness fills one's soul with gratitude, followed by the rather miraculous ability to transform other's self-concepts by the brilliant use of Presuppositions. The music continues as the beauty of love is lived.

MEET THE AUTHOR

Frank Reinhardt Morris (b. 1935) has alternately been an ordained minister, chaplain, psychotherapist, philosopher, poet, novelist, scholar, builder, spouse, father, and empirical theorist. The golden thread throughout all the iterations is a man driven to understand human psychology and, in the process, make redemptive contributions.

In this short book, Frank is particularly proud of a breakthrough of new understanding of human consciousness. It turns out that perspectival consciousness joins with the brain/mind's computational abilities and congeals complexity of self, others and phenomena into unified generalizations. This process provides both rational and irrational results – rational with noble Reason and irrational with simplistic and destructive relational results. As Alexander Pope poetically said, *"A little learning is a dangerous thing. Drink deeply or taste not the Pieria Spring: There shallow draughts intoxicate the brain, and drinking largely sobers us again."*

Since 1975, Frank, and his sterling partner Dix, have been co-therapists using a collage of therapeutic options with their clients. The options include Transactional Analysis, Gestalt Therapy, Client-Centered Therapy, Hypnotherapy, Neuro-linguistics, body therapies, and Psychoanalysis.

For two decades Dix and Frank held three year Training Groups on modern psychotherapy with professionals and intelligent lay people who desired to understand human nature and become therapeutic with others. Both Frank and Dix are Transactional Analysts.

Liberation Psychotherapy has five emphases: SASHET emotions, understanding the power of Abandonment, Life Force Energy, the Modular Mind, and linguistic usage of Presuppositions.

Frank has two children by a previous marriage: John Mark Morris who is an executive in data storage and an inventor with over forty patents, and Jill Marie Morris who owns pet businesses in California and Florida. Dix has a daughter, Leigh Kahn, who is a Marketing Research Consultant for a range of companies in the United States. The extended family of Frank and Dix includes four grandchildren, three great-grand-children and friends across the country.

Frank and Dix retired in Colorado, are deeply in love, and spend senior years studying nature, reading, and continuing to be a resource for others.

This is Frank's tenth book and represents the culmination of his lifelong drive to understand humans and devise therapeutic pathways.

BOOKS available from: WWW.Amazon.com
& from: WWW.CreateSpace.com

**The Evolutionary Logic
Of
Liberation Psychotherapy**
Human Nature in the Twenty-First Century
By Frank R. Morris – 2016

Freedom through Psychotherapy
For Self-Analysis & How to Transform Others
By Frank R. Morris & Dix *Lela Gescheidle* Morris

TELL 'EM WHO THEY ARE
How Grandparents Change the World,
One Person a Time / By Frank R. Morris

How Freud Changed World Civilization
By Frank R. Morris

MEMOIRS:
My Hopscotch Journey by Dix *Lela Gescheidle* Morris
A Lifelong Passion by Frank R. Morris

BOOKS by Frank R. Morris at: WWW.LULU.com

Liberation Psychotherapy, An Empirical System

Poisonous Ideologies and Their Antidotes

The Freudian Labyrinth

NOVELS: *Black Opal   &   Slavery Unshackled*

An insightful description of six emotions and Darwin's ideas about expressing those emotions, described and illustrated by the author, will lead a reader on the pathway to a deeper understanding of oneself and the ensuing emotional freedom. Very useful new ideas for individuals, therapists, and classroom teachers.
Mary Kay Walsh,
Educator

* * * * *

Frank Morris shares his life's work, which is a blue-print for emotional and psychological health. The text asks: Can a person learn and acquire the tools to build joy and soul into themselves? The overview is powerful evidence that we can!
It is Mastery.
Christopher Channer
Channer Investment Management